Dark Way Down
by
Lauren Parker

Advance Praise for *Dark Way Down*

"Dark Way Down is a fantastical deadhead-dad hangover dream that shoots across the Southwest, a jagged journey of longing, road food, cocaine and booze. If David Bowie only knew. Maybe he does."
—Jack Bouleware, music journalist, co-founder of Litquake, and author of *Gimme Something Better*

"All perversity and prayer, with lines like 'kisses that sound like creaks of leather' or 'I don't have energy enough to be demon anymore,' *Dark Way Down* is a poetic road trip that moves from safety to uncertainty and discovery with glee."
—Tomas Moniz, author of *All Friends Are Necessary*

"The loss of a generational talent like David Bowie leaves a hole in us, and into that hole falls all our feelings about their work and all the people we felt it with. The only cure, naturally, is more good art. Hold *Dark Way Down* to the place where you ache."
—Meg Elison, Locus Award-winning author of *Big Girl*

"Parker takes us on a cocaine-fueled road trip on the knife edge of an arid dystopia, down back roads so vividly painted you can feel the grind of the dust in your teeth. With David Bowie on the radio, David Bowie in the atmosphere, David Bowie as her co-pilot, Parker pulls us from a heat baked America populated by the desiccated souls of a world gone by, to the stardust sparkle of the cosmos looming above. It's dark and it's gritty, and somehow, somehow it's all about love."
—Noah Sanders, editor and curator of *The Racket*

"Dark Way Down is a wolf howling into the unknown, it propels you on an expertly crafted poetic escape, booming rock songs in your ears, red dirt and dust of the mysteries of universe in your fingernails and hair, wild, queer, and deeply moving. This poetry collection made me want to drink again (don't worry I won't), it made me miss gin, whiskey, and tequila. Parker's poems intimately present you with the seductive way meat can leave bone, the beauty, the pain, and that beauty and pain can taste delicious. This is a must read collection from a rockstar of the Bay Area literary world."

—Baruch Porras Hernandez, author of *Tiny Baruch, I Miss You Delicate* and *Lovers of the Deep Fried Circle*

Dark
Way
Down

Lauren Parker

Parker, Lauren / author

Dark Way Down / Lauren Parker

Poems

ISBN: 979-8-9869524-8-2

Edited by: Jude Marr
Book Design: Amanda McLeod
Cover Art: Valeriia Neganova via Unsplash
Cover Design: Amanda McLeod

PUBLISHER
Animal Heart Press
1854 Hendersonville Rd. Ste A
PMB 211
Asheville, NC 28803
www.animalheartpress.net

For the Thin White Duke. You know what you did.

Contents

Wild is the Wind

Prologue

In the fall of 1975, David Bowie was at the peak of his cocaine addiction. He was barely eating, reading occult books, and becoming more and more incoherent. He gave alarming interviews. And he made an iconic album, *Station to Station*. The songs are erratic and dark, the album very bound to place. The main character, Bowie's last character, the Thin White Duke, is a dark and suited tyrant, a charismatic but dangerous charlatan who stalked his creator sober.

In the summer of 2020, all I could do was listen to David Bowie and write poems. In the endless stretch of lockdown I was on a mental journey through the desert, rambling down the highway, and reflecting on relationships and character. For the Thin White Duke, I imagined a lesbian daughter.

This collection, a speculative continuation of *Station to Station*, came from my pensive daydreams out of Dodge. In these poems, the Daughter of the Duke, a mixed-up queering of bygone relics and Casanova, drives a rickety Chevelle from Bel Air to the Mesas of New Mexico seeking the place where her father was last seen. This is what she found.

Daughter of the Duke

Kingship

Train's coming, slows along the tracks outta town
chug, stretch, high pitched loud warning
is it a train, the whip of blades overhead?
You are fauna, run, run forever
you are flora, curl under
or
be resilient enough
to spring back
leaves opening like a fist
welcome to my debut, so nice of you to wear gloves & tails
the Daughter of the Thin White Duke.

Foundation

Meet him, the dearly departed, dirty daddy
raw monger of something like love, something like flame
I flick the lighter, over & over, she asks me if I ever
worry I'll catch fire
but what fire could burn something this cold?

She & I don't talk anymore, she's pinned to the roof
in the visor, I carry her everywhere & she'll never know

Splendor

I love you far, I love you deep, love on a horizon line
retreating.

I have learned to drive the hard way, hitch,
hike, grabbing the wheel from the drunks
that would have me, steering as unwelcome fingers
wet themselves with my fear
but I stay between two lines, one broke, borders
deteriorated, but I keep to the bowed center of the lane
until I run out of gas, until I run out of the car

I missed the greyhound, hateful,
checking my watch like a scroll, counting
down the seconds to Haley's comet,
tracing the fire in the sky.

Victory

Gosh, we are jolly, fingers crammed against piano keys
in the smokiest bar left in Los Angeles, tell nobody
souls are made up, I never had one.

My mother might have, granules of Kether
she's wilted, a kind voice in the head.

She loved this song, plates of fries used as ashtrays
we howl over the karaoke machine.

Beauty

Do you understand the initial wobble
Of thick white lines, cut thinner
Cut disappearing
Fade & fade & fade to gossamer?
You can never disappear, you restrain
You refine, chop chop, razor blade
Long inhale, you forget what food tastes like
What fullness does to the stomach, you turn down
Never off.

Kindness

It's been a long journey, this far
So much more left to go, to find
The site of the death of a spaceman
He's the last one, the rumored form.

Will we get there, will we get there?
I crawl south, dragging an American canon.

Understanding

We are ten minutes in & you don't know a damn
I'm drinking Florida Water & eating chalk
we are doldrum magic, the flame on black candles
in the backyard of a Bel Air house, stolen magic.

The Thin White Duke, barely a noble
largely a poet, drowning in the whitecaps
water turned to powder, distrust in lungs
we both pound on the keys, white keys
minor keys, you have nothing better to do
let me save

you

drive like a demon, I was the afterthought of a
man's darkest days, soaked in cocaine & streetlight
more of my DNA is daddy reaching out to Mars
than reaching to the stars within.

Wisdom

drive   like   a   demon

Coast   like   a   ghost

It's just me & these roads & this desert
& the memory of my mother, the Duke's Dartboard
eye poked out & snorted up.

We all become our fathers, our mothers become our victims.

Crown

Do the dead interest themselves in the affairs of the living?
Listen to the train. Closer now.

4

Station to Station

The Duke is Dead

We start at the end
the duke is dead, the voice
is my radio, the one from the car
he left me, a shambled wreck.

In the rearview, a slit of eye
I slick back my hair, straighten my collar
my black suit touches the leather
seat, the crinkle of my shirt
like petals clutched, the seat
has no headrest, if I crash I'm crushed.

You are smoke in my mouth, you are
the fertile promise of ash, of the next
the afternow, the whine of the engine
calls out over the wild wind.

I am bold against the desert, white
& black, he left me the suit
he left me the car, he left me
stardust to assemble together.

There is frost on my fingers
& white dust in my pockets
we are in this together, you & me
will you join me to find the moon
the crescent knife hanging in fame.

Let's run away, girl, let's run from this
my daddy's a demon & he can help us
look at this car he left me, look at this suit
Don't I look like I can take care of you?

With your kiss, my life begins.

Lust for Life

I know a woman who mixes the clay dirt
of Arizona with water & paints her lips.
I've done your chart, she says, flipping
Ephemeris, drawing glyphs on the mirror
in eyeliner, the only sound I can hear
is the scrape of the pages against each other.

My father didn't call me all at once
grains of him slipped into me through
coffee grounds, the sweet of Vermouth

She says I won't be happy until I find him
Saturn is up to no good here, it rules you.
I lick at her snot so full of crystal it shines
in the candlelight, she pulls back laughing
You'll be gone in the morning, don't ruin it with vice.
I can feel the burn of the keys in my pocket
they fit in the '72 Chevelle parked in front
of her building. I've been looking for a reason
to get gone. I've been drawing in my sleep
eyes in the sky, like searchlights
I know he landed there, in the sagebrush
& rambled his way to Los Angeles
I wear his hat now, she takes the eyeliner
& draws the glyph of Saturn, *for where you're going*
Hagalaz, for who you are.
She has marked me since we met,
& when she finally sleeps with the tang of white
wine on her lips, I put on my
hat, his hat, our hat to go.
I leave Bel Air with the sun chasing me out.

Golden Years

Highway Pearls

Look at that sky,
muddied red & orange, lashes of gold
the road howls against the engine
we've run out of town, not out of road
me & the Duke, *in the back of a dream car twenty foot long, girl.*

There's got to be a god
high on coke cut with the brim of a fedora
the lines in the road rush & rush & warp & wad
twisting & compressed with the heat of the day
until they look whole & ornamental
torn from someone's neck, sweat beads
along the hollow of my throat
run for the shadows.

Hundreds of miles yet to New Mexico, noon
is a loud swelter, cooled only when I pull
off & into a concrete bar called the Orion's Belt
no windows, dark & cool as an ice chest
that there's anything out here is a miracle
gotta be a god.

In walked luck & you looked in time
wearing white shirt, black vest, grit
pressed into the lines of my face
all I want is water, all they have is tequila
& cups of ice I let sit on the counter
until enough liquid forms from the diamonds
blue in the neon light.

The jukebox is an old thing, rattling merrily
the volume rattling my glass
sleek with sweat on the wood of the bar
sniffle, there's a bathroom if I need it
be a god.

The bartender looks like Elvis,
the ash like the dust off the car

Got far to go? Bar Elvis puts
another glass of ice in front of me.
The whites in my eyes reflected
like the lines of the highway.

The sweat, pearled, now makes
my clothes stick to me & chill
my hands start to shake.
I order tequila this time, a plate of fries
a few single cigarettes, they offer me
shots in tubes that smell like apple & everclear.

I think I could die here, in the cool blue light
of this bar in this town, in black slacks
sipping tequila & eating french fries
until they drag me out of here like a stool
when they close up.

The Duke whispers in a mellow hiss
Don't you have some shadows to chase?
Do you have a thousand years to spend?

There's gotta be a god, there's gotta be, god a be.

Always Crashing in the Same Car

The transmission towers look like gowns
arms flung out like laundry against the land.
I climb one, rung over rung, I can hear the electricity
in my teeth, every hair standing like weeds in summer.

If they ever hang me, let it be from here
wind on my face & in my hair
until I erode away like a crag.
The few times I'm a man & nothing else
not alien not daughter not Urantian urchin
making myth out of bar room gossip.

I could turn myself into animals once
but it never healed all the way.
I lost the tips of these three fingers
jackrabbit.
Lost the heel of my right foot
salamander.
Lost the most fragile pieces of my mind
it goes on all fours.

Never heal all the way.

Save Me, Saint Iggy

Bless Me, Saint Iggy!
I repent of my sins against you
& rock n' roll.
Make me an instrument of your chaos.
Where there is mediocrity, let me sow love,
where there is complacency, pardon
where there is doubt, faith,
where there is despair, rage,
where there is darkness, darkness still,
where there is folly, wisdom.
O, Divine Disaster, grant that I may not so much seek
to be consoled
as to console,
not so much to find danger
as to be dangerous,
not so much to be loved,
as to love;
for it is in taking that we receive,
it is in pardoning that we are foolish,
it is in dyking that we awake to eternal life.

Oh, great Goddess of the Gas Station Tree line
emerging from sigil & storm
called with wunjo & algiz & spit & want
You have made me & remade me,
& you have bestowed on me
all the good things I possess,
& still I do not know you
& I will throw the bones still inside you.
I have not yet done that
for which I was made.
Every spell I ever cast was about a girl
with a want so solid
stony
I can call a woman to me with a stick & a palmful of dirt.

Teach me to seek divinity,
for I cannot seek you
unless you teach me,
or find you
unless you show yourself to me.
Let me seek you in my desire,
let me desire you in my seeking.
Let me find you by loving you,
Let me love you when I find you.

Silver Screen

We pulled into the drive-in with dry mouths
the last mile I had listed all the ways
in which I was better than anyone you had ever
loved, & I think you'd gotten tired of me
the heat making your hair lose its curl.

Cacti had been the only arms outstretched to us
bushy heaps of things, their claws blooming
I play the Stooges loudly, Iggy shouting into the wind
unraveling celluloid, the saint that blesses us.

The wind wets your eyes & bleeds your lipstick
I'd still kiss you.

We pulled into the drive-in, & the boy taking money
& running the card machine looks like a young Elvis
hair black & oily, slick & strong
I worry he'll try & take you from me, but you don't even
blink at him, you blink at Bowie on the screen.

He's willowed, stitched in, a shadow under a hat
the strange thing about movies is that they don't tell you anything.
We sip our Cokes, the first fluid we've drunk that isn't each other
in 60 miles, sun setting, I put my arm around you.
We are a movie about a movie, shadows over a brilliant screen
the funny thing about movies is they never tell you anything.

We spend the night in the car, parked in the lot, stretched
across the bench seats of my inherited Chevelle
seeking my inherited past.

Daddy Duke's mouth curls as he says,
Are you a family man, a man should spend time with his family.
I feel my way down the highway, looking for my family
Daddy Duke, Daddy Dyke,
he floats across the screen, I float across the desert.

A guy like you wouldn't understand a guy like me.

Word on a Wing

Attack of the T-Rex

I hate having a body.
I press on my eyes until patterns bloom
like an acid trip, browns against blacks
that lighten into a headache
when I hurt I feel less human.

The highway is guarded by dinosaurs
stone statues to entertain children.
Enough to toss a dollar in a ticket machine
to run across pavement & the frozen
likeness of ancient raptors, cartooned
for easy recognition, mark it off the sheet of paper
take your photos, watch the shadows grow & shrink.

I throw my arms up, they creak with hangover
my sweat is mostly gin, but I can make my shadow
reach out its Tyrannous arms, its Tyrant King teeth.
Shadow as black as a star, rigid as the teeth of a
Fuhrer, feathers as preened as ornate lapels.
My footsteps clack like medals of honor, & you
let my Saturn snatch & catch, like a firefly in a jar.

You list all the dinosaurs you can name, *herbivores*
you like all the ones that are gentle.
My mouth tastes like meat & cigarettes.
I press on my eyes.

No Semis Under Canopy

I take a job at a bar on the Arizona border
car broke down & I broke down
got sick of marking the miles & taking
the long way. Just for a month, maybe two
easy enough to grease my hair & button
up my vest at the old man's bar.
& that's the best kind they make
where I remind them all of someone they knew
long ago, which means they never really knew her at all.

The Stardust Lounge is a sad sight.
A beautiful ruin, everything in it sagging & greased
like the smile of someone who's lived a long time
& lost everything on a gamble.
My baby works at the chicken restaurant across
the street, & when our shifts end
even though our feet hurt, we dance
under the one stoplight, me cast in red
her in green.

There's a poster in the window
of the theatre, where they've written
a musical of The Man Who Fell to Earth
COMING SOON faded into the white border.
The Duke's face the same as mine, the
points of our hats align.
He is longer & thinner, shadow man
I am coming soon, weaving my way through
towns & stretches of bewitched landscape.

I'm not good at sitting still
I fill cups, pick at cuticles
put ache in my heart.
Placing something inside
stones on stones, damming up
dammed myself in, damn.
I have to remember how to feel.

Practice sadness, look in the mirror
& work the muscles in my face to show
anything. I'm as numb as I started
the truckers know us now & don't
even honk when we kiss over the bar
your eyes are still bright when they see me.

Did you always live like this?
She asks me, as I count my cut, enough
to finally fix the roof, half what we need
for the brakes, & I cannot remember
a time before now as I pass cash from
one hand to the other, pass drugs
from one hand to my mouth, I try to
remember some before time, wet with joy.

Zzyzx

100 miles to Vegas, I can see the lights from here
the world has never been foggier, than through shots of everclear.

Mojave

The desert & the sky have the same effect
you can't judge the distance
you can reach out & touch everything

you reach out to collect every star & I fill your pockets
with change & say, *stars*
don't exchange like they used to.

You tell me that you can tell the difference between
mountains & hills with one special trick
If you can see the top, it's not a mountain.

& even if I didn't have a spaceship to catch
or a man waiting on me in the wild of the Mesa
I would consider it worth it
                                to ride off into the lush
                                        & crowded desert
with you.

TVC 15

Sons of a Silent Age

This is the part where I'm supposed to talk about how
I love you when you're shy & small & don't hurt me
with how brightly you shine, but I would rip my skin off
for the most mundane, boring, mourning breath
hashbrown-stuck-in-teeth moments. I want to be around
when you forget you need me, shoulders back
sun beaming off your collar bones, I wish I had enough
for you, not hollow heart, not hollow.

When you can't feel a damn thing, all you want is to be
something, to a beautiful girl like you.

You sound like the peeling
of velvet over a bare shoulder
fingers fumbling with sleeves
& dress hitting hips, hitting floor
I'm trapped in this chair wanting you.

We lay out blankets on the hood of the Chevelle
& sleep there on nights when it's not too cold
could catch death, but is it ours?

Desierto de Sonora

Phoenix is always on fire.
The smell of smoke hits a hundred miles outside city limits
the Daughter of the Duke can feel fires
before the house they eat has been built.

It is hard to know where the West becomes wild
where I become wild within it.
This isn't the side effects of the cocaine
I wash my hair in it, dust so white & pale
& thin, gin blooms on your cheeks.

He's in the rear view mirror, but you never see him.
Your eyes glaze over like he's a thing I made up.

The saguaro wear their flower crowns
a landscape of arms ready to hold me down.
We ate their fruit in Tuscan, I drank so much
tequila I saw a series of eyes in the sky.
Blinking & twinkling, lashes trailing stardust.
You drank so much you just looked at me & cried.

Suntanned, Windblown

To remove the skin of a rabbit, you cut a hole
in the back & tear, working your fingers under
the fur & out like you're ripping open a package
of taffies at the shore, the salty sea air making your hair
curl, be quick, quick as the thing, the hard part is always the head.

To remove the skin of a deer, you have to go slowly.
Technique is important, keep your eye on the knife
not on the iron hooks hanging from the ceiling.
Don't let the clink of chains fill your head.
Start at the back leg, follow the tendons.
Learn the release of skin separating from muscle
from fat, split it, like the back of the leg
is coated in the most erotic of stockings.

A bear is a bit like a human, you start at the wrist
the curl of the paw outstretched, handshake.
Split the fur like parting a sea, seam on seam on seam
meet at the throat, jaw, snout, highways of the body.

The meat will glisten too, pink & white
soft angelic like Easter lilies. You'll be surprised
at how the meat is stored, the legs mostly bone
cut knuckles, snap tibia, the symmetry will rock you to sleep.

When you cut off your own skin, you won't be able
to just tear open & out, snap a leg bone after
gliding through tendons, careful to avoid the rump meat.
It doesn't begin with the knife, it begins in the car, day
four, two more than the map said because you're lost.
So incredibly lost, & your car is a classic Chevelle
not built for long trips, & the crook of the neck
of the girl you love is louder than the radio.

You pull & tug at your exterior in the hotel rooms, at the sites
where she runs out & says *take my picture*
& you pretend that the camera is the eye you
see her through, the concave glass lens is the thing

that sees her the most, stark, arms out, shadow among cacti.
She can feel everything, her sides pushed in from
the world, & you stand with your camera
& your skin worked off with a knife, limp in your
hands, limp in the heat, praying she'll eat you or wear you.

The Dowsing Rod

I've dug so much out of the Earth
it lives under my nails & you hold them
cupped, across the table of a Denny's
hashbrowns steaming up like fire season.
All I want is a cigarette.

Here we clarify the Daughter of the Duke
a bundle of cocaine jitters skipping shadow
to shadow, slick as ice.

Glacier formed under my feet,
my shoulders dusted with snow
& now I can't keep it in the glass.
Everything turns to liquid in my hands.

Gallup, NM

Someone call a priest.

The car won't make it out of here
it is laid to rest in the sacred lot
Sundance Motors, the ghost
coasts no more, & we are
on foot, on bus, sleek railriders
of the Greyhound system.

She has started praying at night
& stealing out for phone calls.

I don't sleep anymore, he talks too loud
the Thin White Duke is disappointed
in me, again, I am not the daughter
not the priest, I use her eyeliner to
write my own magic, & she pretends
to still find my glyphs & symbols
enchanting. It's all broken now
all the spells are crumpled & empty.

The light of the day's oranges & dusty
beiges have moved from romantic to rust.

Someone call a priest.

If the devil don't dance, teach him.
I dance by myself in streetlights now
just me & the demon & the stars
she's let fall from her pockets & I scoop
into a pile to see if I have enough for cigarettes.
Stars don't exchange like they used to.

Her bright eyes are dull now, too much want
not enough need
of me.
There's home to go back to, we're both

running the same race.
Her running back, me running on.

Petroglyph, I remove bits & bits
to the messages underneath, picking
at skin until I hear the call.

Someone call a priest.

Stay

Horizon Line

This is one of those places
that's nowhere near the ocean
& only serves seafood
poor curdled octopi
tentacle muddy brown
embarrassed purple-red.

Is this how I would boil
hands reaching up & out of the pot
my meat blooming?

The liquid runs clear, no pink
holes pinpricked to let the broth in.

The Girl on the Back of the Bike

I roll my cigarettes with pages
from the mini bibles the street pastors
cram into our arms on college campuses
& my tongue coats with ink.

I press my tongue to you
leaving tattoos of inhaled verse
the sermons of Paul are ash in my mouth
Matthew 8:5-13 shines coal black
lamp black
boot black
kisses that sound like the creak of leather.

Organic Ripe Fruit Grown Here

It's the sign as large as a two story house
in the shape of a talking strawberry.
The seeds cut into flat red flesh
holes to let the wind through.
The stand has avocados & persimmons.

I finally asked you why you came with me
to find a man who no longer exists
& who might never have been at all.
A dyke with a quick tongue in an old suit
in an old car, with a torn up route.

We are following the dregs of a man
who swore up & down he was there
when he wasn't, specter hands
echo voice, a fog a long way out.

But when you call me *priest* in the night
I feel the ridges & rods of alien want.
I am better than queen, better than king.
I hold the magic that makes you mine.

You descend the steps of the grimy hotel
we've spent four days in, your dress stained
& collar yellowed & still you look
like you're hopping into a limo with someone
far better than me, & I'd kill any man who
thought he had done the work to earn you.

I have memorized this hotel room.
Every crease of the wallpaper
we have been here years now,
you laugh & say we just got here.
I curl up in that, time always feels longer
& longer, nothing goes by fast enough.

The light from the hallway reaches under the door

around the line of the door jamb, I don't
know how to not put on my hat & leave in the night.

You cast your magic in your own way
piling dishes in front of the door so I can't go
so I fall asleep on the floor, the cracks of light
in my eyes, & think of your spell.

When is a door not a door?
When it's ajar.

Rip Torn

Everyone wants to be a starchild
it folds in on me as I drag it across the desert.
I don't know if everyone would lose the taste for it
or if I'm just poorly chosen.
Breath coated with peppers & milk
I resent it all anyhow.

The heat of the night hurts more than
the heat of the day, where we cannot press
against each other because the sky pressed
too hard against us. Our clothes are limp.

I am not good at knowing where I am.
Dreams smear into the day, the horizon
sometimes behind me & I'm driving
off the end of the Earth, I'm forever zoomed
out unless I'm drunk, unless I'm watching your
leg pull itself out of hotel sheets, catching your calf
in my bare hand, like pinning the wing of a bat.
When I remember myself I want to unfold every fold of you.

All there is left to do is ask the questions I don't want answers to:
       Where is your husband?
       What are your children like?
Their shapes become more clear in the dark.

I can't turn myself down, I can't turn your past off.
Was this just a ramble into the underworld?
My attempt to dig up the heart of man with no
heart, no skin, nothing for me, sweat running into my eyes
the collar of my shirt ringed in yellow.
Did I kidnap you & take you down with me?
Through every scrap of desert I could find?
Just to make you prove that your love was real.
That I was real? A story hitchhiking the audience?

I don't even know what you want, I don't even know what you need

I looked at you, fish eye, seeking my reflection.
But the spaceman is dead, disgraced daughter
of a thin, white thing, drawing pentagrams on
walls & carpets to conjure demons.

Here I am, here you are
priests of something more than the magicians who made us.

I could call upon the sky, collect every star
Dawnbringer, hazy white hair like morning
but after all this way I want to creep into your shadow
fold in the night & let it hold me.

It's a long way home to the Milky Way.

Eulogy for the Milky Way

We buried the Milky Way in red dirt
& saliva, it died in shifts.
Whole stars falling damp at our feet
like porch lights going out after midnight.
Until all that was left was a dark seam
of purples & navies in the sky.

The small ones were delicate, like
leaves settling on the ground.
But the larger ones left welts in the dirt.
Everyone thinks the desert is sand
like it will sift through your hands cleanly
but the American West is dirt & clay
& brush & stars are buried beneath it.

I know, I left them there.

I folded them up in my shirt, & carried
them until my arms gave out.
Dug until my thumbnail came off.
Spat the last of the water within me.

The only home I had, a sudsing froth of
light cresting the sky is
gone
gone
gone.

Daddy was a Fascist

Light a black candle
for Prospero, scry what you can in your gin.
Fallen magicians peddling chintz symbols
nobody's home but the ghosts you wrote.

Slip in & out of shape, what is an alien
but a foreigner, Malkuth wrinkled against
the shape of him.

Control seems safe while delirious
arms out, contorting from spinning.
All you want is someone to clamp their hands
around you, the lines are porous between
me & you, & you've melted into air
thin air, thin Duke air.

Slick back your hair to keep your head on
fit your trousers so you can't run away
keep the vest tight to keep the psychosis at bay.

Maybe rock stars *are* fascists
petty tyrants of parlor tricks.
Dance with the schizophrenia fast enough so it
can't pin you down, head full of junk
makes you a junkie, makes everyone around you
a widow, watch the fascist move.
Swagger like jagger, you say you don't want freedom
you want the scald of the spotlight & the roar
of a crowd, let the fans kill you
pull you apart, tear your suit, muss your hair.

Fuck you fuck you fuck you fascist
fuck your rock n roll
fuck the grains of stardust in your hair.

Tidy everything up, Duke.
Collect the wax of those candles, Dad.

Create widows of us all.
The demon eats from the inside.
You are exotic food, sold your soul
wanted to be a lord, remain
a Bastard son, & now that's all you make.

The rot begins in the marrow, the coil
of pulp in your teeth, it roosts.
Builds an empire, makes pedestals
of plaster, death to the rock star
death to the magician
death to the Duke.
Charms overthrown in solemn temples.

I have my dukedom got, & pardon'd the deceiver.

Poker Dice

Be slight.
Be hand.
Be of yourself.
Be in the one place that has air conditioning
in temperatures so hot
you can hear the sizzle of your own skin.

Once I could never be down
talked so long my jaw ached & voice gave out.
Up all night. Holding onto my girl
like she could run away at any moment.

The casino is bright against your face
the reds & blues muted on you like a flush.
You brighten up at civilization.
It makes me hate you for not needing my wilderness.

We haven't paid for a drink in 247 miles
& we won't start now, as we pluck martinis
off trays like we're picking the olives ourselves.

When the blue & red of the casino lights
become the blue & red of the cop cars
we know it's time to close out.

Wild is the Wind

Only a charlatan will hand you a cooked
& calloused secret, one seared on all
sides & tell you it's raw & bloody.
& daddy told secrets so well done
you could hear the sear off the meat.

Sun is the space between shadows.

Once there were mountains, mountains & the crow of lovebirds.
Once I called you to me & you came—no flinch, just fate.
You took off, leaving stars in my pockets, not even a word
you're too gone to be grateful, it's too late, too late.

The Man Who Fell to Earth

Daddy was a shooting star
Mama always said, her fingernail painted
dark as she traced his map across the sky.
& I thought I wouldn't be another woman
holding her child in the back seat
tracing the story of a man she don't have.

It is so hard to face the West,
the setting sun gets dust in your eyes
setting son, one & done.

Imagine it from where I stand
the majesty of nothing to fall
on my knees, my mouth full of dirt.

Imagine not the fall but the hit
body against water as hard as stone.
Ribs fractured, an arm shattered, prolly two.
The mouth open screaming into the rush of air
so fast that you can't inhale it.
Now full with water, undrinkable water
sea receives you in harsh arms.

The mountains were cliffs over
the raging dirt ocean, waves of
volcanic rock & red clay.

Now I wonder how it was to land on Earth.
Brown as Saturn, spiked grass a sharp meadow.
Red smudges on white clothes,
toothy mountains swallowing you
your mouth dry as a canyon, dust
where your blood should be, dust
where your bones once were.

I dreamed of water, I found it in whiskey
I found it in the tang of forever.

Even an alien, a true fish of space
slick & sleek & slithering
wading through stars
shatters like jelly jars.
You know you're alive with the wet
sound of meat, not before
in the gasping struggle of fall
you forget your body, forget limbs
they could turn into rain & fall away.

I am all the water I can carry.

Everyone goes on about their day
some don't even look up when the ground
shakes, ain't no rescue coming.

Saturn turns on a dime, ringed
the future is a stern place, priest
keep your stars in your pockets.

Gasp like a fish in the desert
the roads & lands pocked
with rivers long dry.

All that's left.

All that's left to do is
pray for rain.

Miranda

Life is cost, throwing good years after bad
why make more of it, why shovel out bits of
yourself to create a monument to all you haven't done?

I have so many questions for my father.
Do all ships rock like they are being tossed in waves?
Did you hold your breath when you land?
Are you not my father, Duke?
Shouldn't I look into my face & see you
winking back like the stars?

The seams of your waistcoat have snagged
on brush & cacti, leaving a trail
of stories unwinding, voice swallowed.

If I planted my feet & called your name
would a storm come churning through
the endless sky? Do spaceships sound
like helicopters? Churning & sloped in hover?

Does it sound like a man afraid to say
his own name aloud
afraid of what it will summon?

Date with the Duke

This is the part where you ask me
why my back is against the tire
of a car I stole from a town
I'll never know the name of
every word a curse sealed in spit
like popping a cork on a bottle
of spirits I didn't summon.

What was the search all for?
Torn up clothes, white shirt with pit stains
the sort of yellowed brown you'll never get out.

Do I really love my father to be this dehydrated in the desert?

My back is against the tire, my clothes in tatters
my throat burned out from liquor because I miss the father
I never had, & resent the one I did have
& they are the same person & different people.

I can see him over me, hair red
teeth lined in black
waiting for me to be one more woman
to crawl inside his hologram
to fall into his gossamer.

If I don't get water soon, I'll be the drunk I was destined to.

Be, My Baby

Call me Duke, I say
dirt trails behind me where snow once fell.
Magic doesn't remember me now
no element hears my voice but the heavy
cling of fucking Earth.

Duke, huh?
You're beautiful, of course you are
it used to be that I'd look at you
& think
What is she going to try to take from me
but I already know I'll be the one that eats you
like Kronos, mighty Saturn, swallowing joy
legacy to fuel himself
back when eternity was possible
back when you'd kill a son to prove a point.

What of a son that kills himself
walking in sacred circles in the desert
Isaac gone rogue, what sheep do you have to replace me?

You are beautiful & you have water
& the sort of kind eyes I would darken for fun
so that the hint of my shadow would make you shake
so that you'd sell your soul at the crossroads to me
I don't have the energy to be a demon anymore.

I back away from you without drinking anything.

Lazarus

Does every queer have to fall to their knees in the desert
under the stars, & beg the star man to love them?
Does every queer immolate in sadness?
Eat themselves up to remember taste?
Pull everything off to verify what's underneath?
What can't be tampered with?

I lay out in the desert
legs part like lips, limbs peeled up
pressed down between the ground
& the sky, like a specimen for notation.

I try to shift to something more adapted to survive
coyote, jack rabbit, road runner
but I am no magician, no priest, no.

The parts of the Duke that I loved are gone
the Duke is dead, & the duke is dead within me
I vomit whole parts of him, liquid hydrogen splatters
red dirt, work out solid helium that thuds as it
cuts out of me, cold cauterizing.
I could make a new me, & new Duke
a new star man, give me time, just give me time.

I lay out in the desert
I lay out in the desert
I am alone.

Black Star

Kindred ghosts, I'm his echo
warped, faded vapor
fuck them so you live on
in their tongues, their nerves, write
yourself into their DNA, until all they
do just makes more of you.

The sea holds the sky's memories like
myth, like molecules, kept in jars.

What are jellyfish but wet, resilient stars?
What are whales but comets?
Sea. The sky's dark mirror.

Eyes wet & shining,
concave mirror, stumble backward groping the ground
for home, you don't know if you want the Earth to
let you go or hold you down, so close your heartbeat
syncs to roots cracking dirt open
everything is digging, palms blushed with dirt.

I want & ache & ache & know.
I feel so much more on this caustic rock.
Father, help me, I am broken windows
blown out the house.

I want to know this town. I want to know it to the ground.
Hungry for fire & ash
bite coal into diamond, spit them into caves.

Infinite Saturn, when a man sees his
black star, he knows his time has come.
I am scanning the skies to see the omens
of my father, to read the crumbs of stars
wrung out & cracked, Ormen slithering
sailing longship casting night over desert.

As a child I remember eating every lightning bug I could catch.
Smashing their bodies in my mouth
breaking them open & running through the dark
glowing carnelian, chartreuse
vibrant as glass bottles.
Small spots of fire in the night, borealis
collecting the bodies the lamp killed
with love & lust for its light.
How do you nurture a starseed?
How do you bury the Starman?

Eat them, eat them fast.
Feel the stars in your belly
glow bright as star seed.
I could feel him in me, in the shape of my
hands, in the shape of my hunger.

Don't you know

you're life itself?

Acknowledgements

"Miranda" was originally published in *Strange Horizons*, and "Mojave" was originally published in *Quiet Lightning*. "Sunburned, Windblown" was originally published in *The Racket* and then featured again by poet laureate Kim Schuck as part of the San Francisco Library's Poem a Day project.

I want to thank every person who had to listen to me talk about this book. I want to thank John Elison for driving me to New Mexico to write poems and for thoughtful edits throughout this process—you watched it take form. I want to thank Matt Carney for producing the audiobook and being an excellent friend. I want to thank Animal Heart Press, especially my fantastic editor Jude Marr, for their tireless devotion to every thought I had, no matter how inconvenient the time zone, and for treating this book like a friend. I cannot thank you all enough.

I want to thank Noah Sanders, Meg Elison, Tomas Moniz, Baruch Porras Hernandez, and Jack Bouleware for blurbing this book and for being the sorts of writers that inspire me and enrapture me.

I want to thank my mother, who never, not once, said I couldn't do it.

And lastly, I want to thank David Bowie, whose words and whose life inspired this collection. Thanks for being there, even now.

About the Author

Lauren Parker is a fourth generation female breadwinner descended from male charlatans, and thus has grown up to become a very educated liar. She is a writer, zine maker, poet, and visual artist based in Oakland, California. and has written for *The Toast, Strange Horizons, The Racket, Xtra Magazine, Catapult,* and *Autostraddle.* Most of her work discusses the intersection of queer identity, class identity, and regional animism. She's the author of the poetry collection *We Are Now the Thing in the Woods* (Bottlecap Press, 2023) and *Spells for Success* (Simon Element, 2025). She has a newsletter, *Do You Want to Do Some Witchcraft,* where she discusses witchcraft and spooky things, and is the co-owner of Hidden Hand, a metaphysical and witchcraft store.

When she's not writing poems, essays, or thinking too hard about pop culture, she spends time taking trapeze classes, loving her black cats, and trying to be the best friend she can be.

And if the Thin White Duke ever asks about her, tell him she's not dead yet.

www.ingramcontent.com/pod-product-compliance
Lightning Source LLC
LaVergne TN
LVHW051607080426
835510LV00020B/3174